~A BINGO BOOK~

North Carolina Bingo Book

COMPLETE BINGO GAME IN A BOOK

Written By Rebecca Stark

ISBN 978-0-87386-526-5

Educational Books 'n' Bingo

Printed in the U.S.A.

DIRECTIONS

INCLUDED:

List of Terms

Templates for Additional Terms and Clues

2 Clues per Term

30 Unique Bingo Cards

Markers

1. **Either cut apart the book or make copies of ALL the sheets. You might want to make an extra copy of the clue sheets to use for introduction and review. Keep the sheets in an envelope for easy reuse.**

2. Cut apart the call cards with terms and clues.

3. Pass out one bingo card per student. There are enough for a class of 30.

4. Pass out markers. You may cut apart the markers included in this book or use any other small items of your choice.

5. Decide whether or not you will require the entire card to be filled. Requiring the entire card to be filled provides a better review. However, if you have a short time to fill, you may prefer to have them do the just the border or some other format. Tell the class before you begin what is required.

6. There are 50 terms. Read the list before you begin. If there are any terms that have not been covered in class, you may want to read to the students the term and clues before you begin.

7. There is a blank space in the middle of each card. You can instruct the students to use it as a free space or you can write in answers to cover terms not included. Of course, in this case you would create your own clues. (Templates provided.)

8. Shuffle the cards and place them in a pile. Two or three clues are provided for each term. If you plan to play the game with the same group more than once, you might want to choose a different clue for each game. If not, you may choose to use more than one clue.

9. Be sure to keep the cards you have used for the present game in a separate pile. When a student calls, "Bingo," he or she will have to verify that the correct answers are on his or her card AND that the markers were placed in response to the proper questions. Pull out the cards that are on the student's card keeping them in the order they were used in the game. Read each clue as it was given and ask the student to identify the correct answer from his or her card.

10. If the student has the correct answers on the card AND has shown that they were marked in response to the *correct questions,* then that student is the winner and the game is over. If the student does not have the correct answers on the card OR he or she marked the answers in response to *the wrong questions,* then the game continues until there is a proper winner.

11. If you want to play again, reshuffle the cards and begin again.

Have fun!

TERMS INCLUDED

Bath

Battle of Bentonville

Battle of Moores Creek Bridge

Blackbeard

Border(s)

Catawba

Charlotte

Cherokee

Climate

Coastal Plain

County (-ies)

Jefferson Davis

Edward B. Dudley

Durham

Edenton Tea Party

Executive Branch

Flag

Fort Bragg

Gold

Great Dismal Swamp

Great Seal

Great Smoky Mountains

Inner Banks

Andrew Jackson

Andrew Johnson

Judicial Branch

Kitty Hawk

Legislative Branch

Manufacturing (-ture)

Motto

Mount Mitchell

Mountain Region

New Bern

Nickname

Outer Banks

Pamlico Sound

Piedmont

Plantation

James Polk

Raleigh

Sir Walter Raleigh

Research Triangle

River(s)

Roanoke Island

Tidewater

Trail of Tears

Tuscarora

Union

University of North Carolina

Wilmington

© **Barbara M. Peller**

Additional Terms

Choose as many additional terms as you would like and write them in the squares. Repeat each as desired.
Cut out the squares and randomly distribute them to the class.
Instruct the students to place their square on the center space of their card.

North Carolina Bingo

Clues for Additional Terms

Write three clues for each of your additional terms.

1. _____ 2. 3.	1. _____ 2. 3.
1. _____ 2. 3.	1. _____ 2. 3.
1. _____ 2. 3.	1. _____ 2. 3.

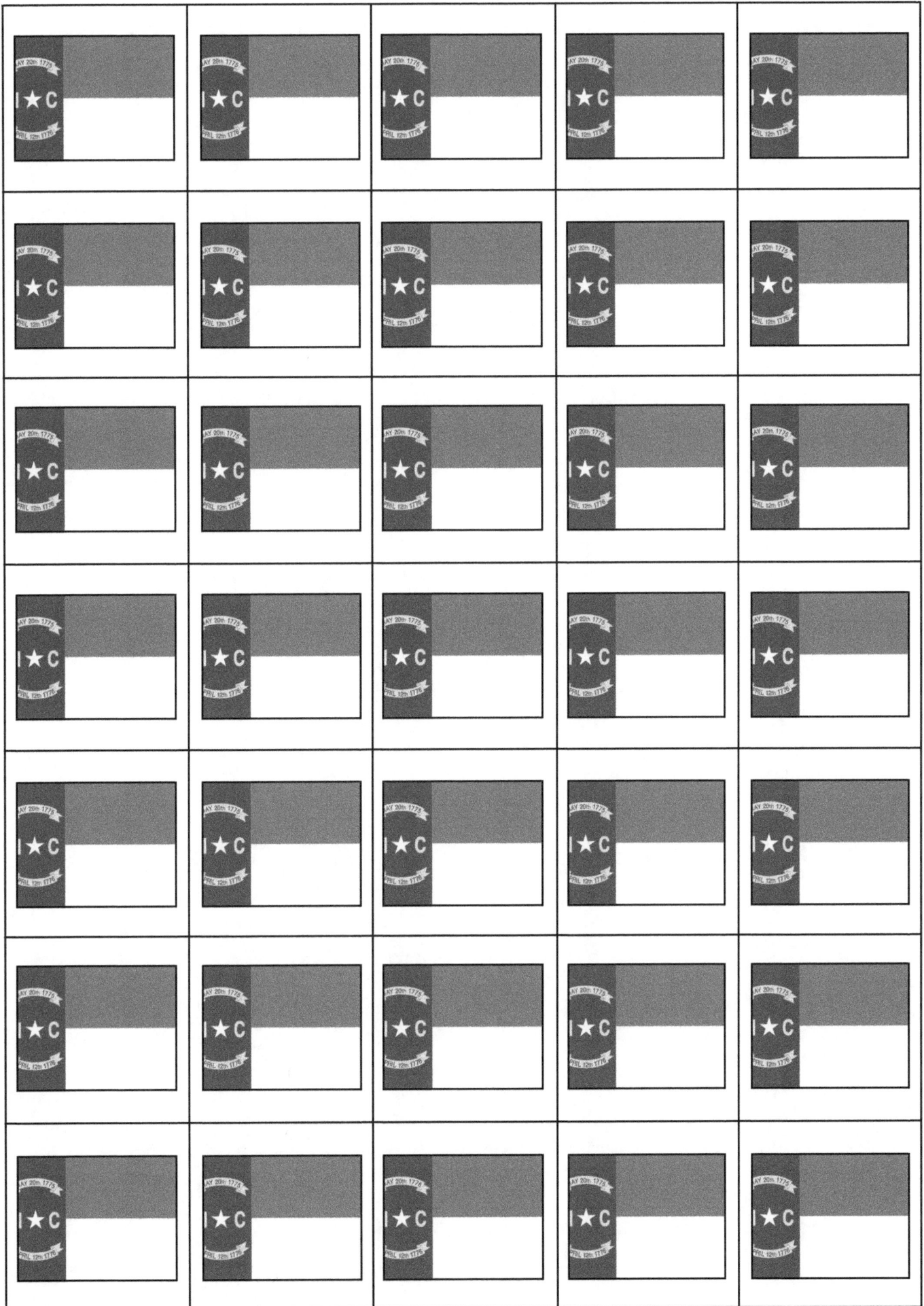

Bath

1. ___ was North Carolina's first town.
2. Founded in 1705, ___ was once considered the colony's capital.

Battle of Bentonville

1. This Civil War battle took place March 19–21, 1865, in rural Johnston County.
2. The Confederates were defeated at the ___. It was the bloodiest battle fought in North Carolina.

Battle of Moores Creek Bridge

1. The ___ was the first battle of the American Revolution to be fought in North Carolina.
2. The ___ was fought on February 27, 1776.

Blackbeard

1. Edward Teach, better known as ___, was a notorious pirate.
2. This pirate once lived near Bath. He was killed off the North Carolina coast in 1718.

Border(s)

1. South Carolina, Georgia, Tennessee, and Virginia ___ North Carolina.
2. The Atlantic Ocean ___ North Carolina on the east.

Catawba

1. The ___ were once a powerful Siouan tribe of the Southeast. They are also known as the Iswa.
2. The reservation of the ___ Indian Nation is along the border of North and South Carolina near Rock Hill, South Carolina.

Charlotte

1. ___ is the largest city in North Carolina. It is the county seat of Mecklenburg County.
2. The NASCAR Hall of Fame is in ___.

Cherokee

1. The ___ are part of the Iroquoian language family.
2. The 56,000-acre Qualla Boundary in western North Carolina is home to the Eastern Band of ___ Indians. It is adjacent to the Great Smoky Mountains National Park.

Climate

1. Much of the state has a humid, subtropical ___.
2. The Coastal Plain has a milder ___ than that of the Appalachian Mountain range in the west.

Coastal Plain

1. The low, flat land along the Atlantic Ocean is called the ___. It is the largest of the three geographic areas and is divided into two parts.
2. The Outer ___ is made up of the Outer Banks and the Tidewater region. The Inner ___ begins west of the Tidewater.

North Carolina Bingo

County (-ies)	**Jefferson Davis**
1. There are 100 ___ in North Carolina. 2. Raleigh, the capital, is mostly in Wake ___. A small portion extends into Durham County.	1. ___ was President of the Confederacy. 2. Although ___ argued against secession, he resigned from the United States Senate and became President of the Confederacy.
Edward B. Dudley	**Durham**
1. ___ was the first popularly elected governor of North Carolina. 2. ___ was governor from 1836 to 1841. Previous governors were elected by the state senate.	1. Along with Raleigh and Chapel Hill, __ is part of the Research Triangle. Duke University is in ___. 2. Much of ___'s growth was attributed to the establishment of a thriving tobacco industry.
Edenton Tea Party	**Executive Branch**
1. A 1774 protest by the women of Edenton became known as the ___. 2. The ___ of 1774 was led by Penelope Barker.	1. The governor is head of the ___. The present-day governor is [fill in]. 2. The ___ of government enforces laws. It comprises the governor, the lieutenant governor, the secretary of state, and several agencies.
Flag	**Fort Bragg**
1. There is a blue field on the left side of the state ___. On the right are 2 bars: a red one on the top and a white on the bottom. 2. Two dates are on the state ___: May 20th, 1775, and April 12th, 1776. They are also on the Great Seal.	1. This large army installation is located mostly in Fayetteville. 2. ___ is named for Confederate general Braxton Bragg and covers over 251 square miles.
Gold	**Great Dismal Swamp**
1. Reed ___ Mine is the site of the first documented find of this mineral in the United States. 2. North Carolina led the nation in ___ production until 1848, when the great rush to California began.	1. The ___ is a marshy area of the Coastal Plain Region of southeastern Virginia and northeastern North Carolina. 2. The ___ National Wildlife Refuge includes over 112,000 acres of forested wetlands.

North Carolina Bingo

Great Seal 1. The female figures on the ___ represent Liberty and Plenty. 2. The state motto, "Esse quam videri," is on the ___.	**Great Smoky Mountains** 1. The ___ National Park is on the border between North Carolina and Tennessee. It is America's most visited national park. 2. The ___ are part of the Southern Appalachian Mountains.
Inner Banks 1. The ___ region is higher and drier than the Outer Banks. The rich, sandy soil here provides excellent farmland. 2. The Sandhills in the southwestern corner of the ___ consist of rolling, sandy hills. This area has the highest elevation of the Coastal Plain.	**Andrew Jackson** 1. Born in Western North Carolina, ___ was the seventh President of the United States. 2. His nickname was "Old Hickory."
Andrew Johnson 1. ___ was the seventeenth President of the United States. He was born in Raleigh in 1808. 2. ___ became President of the United States when President Lincoln was assassinated. He was the only former President to be elected to the U.S. Senate.	**Judicial Branch** 1. The ___ interprets what our laws mean and makes decisions about the laws and those who break them. 2. The ___ is made up of several courts, the highest of which is the state Supreme Court.
Kitty Hawk 1. The state quarter honors the "First Flight" at ___, North Carolina. 2. Orville Wright was riding in the *Flyer* when it made the first successful heavier-than-air, machine-powered flight at ___.	**Legislative Branch** 1. The General Assembly is the ___ of government; it comprises the Senate and the House of Representatives. 2. The ___ makes the laws.
Manufacturing (-ture) 1. The textile industry is the largest ___ sector. 2. The ___ of textiles, tobacco, and furniture are important industries.	**Motto** 1. *"Esse Quam Videri"* is the state ___. 2. The translation of the state is "To be [virtuous] rather than to seem [to be virtuous]."

North Carolina Bingo

Mount Mitchell 1. ___ is in the Black Mountains in the western part of the state. 2. At 6,684 feet, ___ is the highest point in the United States east of the Mississippi.	**Mountain Region** 1. The ___ in the western part of the state is the smallest of the three main geographic regions. 2. The Blue Ridge and Great Smoky Mountains are among the ranges in the ___. Like the other ranges in this western region, they are part of the Appalachians.
New Bern 1. ___ is the second oldest city in the state after Bath. 2. Tryon Palace in ___ was completed in 1770. It served as the first permanent capitol of North Carolina and home to the Tryon family.	**Nickname** 1. North Carolina's ___ is The Tar Heel State. It is also the ___ of the athletic teams of the University of North Carolina at Chapel Hill. 2. The state's ___ probably comes from its production of naval supplies, such as tar, pitch, rosin, and turpentine.
Outer Banks 1. The ___ are a string of barrier islands separated from the mainland by sounds or inlets. Cape Hatteras, Cape Lookout, and Cape Fear are part of the ___. 2. The ___ separate the Currituck Sound, Albemarle Sound, and Pamlico Sound from the Atlantic Ocean.	**Pamlico Sound** 1. ___ is the largest lagoon along the East Coast. The Neuse and Pamlico* rivers flow into the ___ from the west. 2. ___ is separated from the Atlantic Ocean by the Outer Banks. *The Pamlico is the estuary of the Tar River.
Piedmont 1. The ___ lies between the Coastal Plain and the Blue Ridge Mountains. There are many rivers, streams, and waterfalls where the Coastal Plain and the ___ regions meet. 2. The ___ is the most densely populated of the three main geographic regions. It contains the five largest cities.	**Plantation** 1. There are over 200 antebellum ___ homes still standing in the state. 2. Hayes Farm is a historic ___ near Edenton. It belonged to Samuel Johnston, governor of North Carolina from 1787 to 1789.
James Polk 1. ___ was the eleventh President of the United States. 2. This President was born in Mecklenburg County in 1839, but he spent most of his life in Tennessee.	**Raleigh** 1. ___ is the capital and the second largest city in the state. 2. ___, Durham, and Chapel Hill are the main cities of the Research Triangle metropolitan region.
North Carolina Bingo	© **Barbara M. Peller**

Sir Walter Raleigh

1. ___'s first expedition to Roanoke in 1585 failed when the settlers deserted the colony.
2. ___ sent a second, larger expedition to Roanoke in 1587; when he arrived, there were no colonists.

Research Triangle

1. Raleigh, Durham, and Chapel Hill are the major cities of the ___ metropolitan region.
2. The name ___ originally referred to the universities whose research facilities attracted businesses.

River(s)

1. The Neuse, Roanoke, Cape Fear, Tar, and Yadkin are ___ in North Carolina.
2. The Neuse is the longest ___ entirely within North Carolina. It empties into Pamlico Sound.

Roanoke Island

1. ___ is sometimes called the Lost Colony. The fate of the colonists has never been determined.
2. Virginia Dare, the first child born in the Americas to English parents, was born in ___.

Tidewater

1. The area along the coast close to sea level is called the ___. This region has many low-lying wetlands.
2. The Outer Coastal Plain is made up of the Outer Banks and the ___ region. The Pamlico, Albemarle, Currituck, Croatan, Roanoke, Core, and Bogue sounds are in the ___ region.

Trail of Tears

1. The ___ refers to the forced relocation of Native American nations from the Southeast to Indian Territory.
2. The Cherokee called the forced relocation following the Indian Removal Act of 1830 the ___. Many hid in the mountains of North Carolina.

Tuscarora

1. The ___ War was fought from 1711 to 1713. It was a war between the British, Dutch, and German settlers and the ___.
2. Chief Hancock was the leader of the ___.

Union

1. North Carolina became the twelfth state in the ___ when it ratified the Constitution on November 21, 1789.
2. North Carolina seceded from the ___ on May 20, 1861, and joined the Confederacy. It was readmitted on July 4, 1868.

University of North Carolina

1. Founded in 1789, the ___ was the first public university in the United States.
2. Michael Jordan played basketball for the ___ Tar Heels for three seasons.

Wilmington

1. This port city is the county seat of New Hanover County. It was an important Confederate port during the Civil War.
2. The Bellamy Mansion in historic downtown ___ was built between 1859 and 1861.

North Carolina Bingo

Plantation	Bath	Battle of Moores Creek Bridge	Gold	Border(s)
Flag	Battle of Bentonville	Union	Motto	Sir Walter Raleigh
Tuscarora	Manufacturing (-ture)		Outer Banks	University of North Carolina
Trail of Tears	Raleigh	Tidewater	Legislative Branch	Mountain Region
Nickname	Great Smoky Mountains	Durham	River(s)	Andrew Johnson

North Carolina Bingo: Card No. 1

North Carolina Bingo

Trail of Tears	Tuscarora	Andrew Jackson	James Polk	Kitty Hawk
Mountain Region	Edenton Tea Party	Cherokee	Raleigh	New Bern
Coastal Plain	Great Smoky Mountains		Inner Banks	Tidewater
Pamlico Sound	Piedmont	Manufacturing (-ture)	Wilmington	Border(s)
Sir Walter Raleigh	Union	Durham	Flag	River(s)

North Carolina Bingo: Card No. 2

North Carolina Bingo

Great Smoky Mountains	Tidewater	Edenton Tea Party	Legislative Branch	Tuscarora
Mountain Region	Battle of Bentonville	Climate	Bath	Great Seal
Raleigh	Union		New Bern	Blackbeard
Manufacturing (-ture)	Coastal Plain	Nickname	Pamlico Sound	Andrew Jackson
River(s)	County (-ies)	Durham	Wilmington	Kitty Hawk

North Carolina Bingo: Card No. 3

North Carolina Bingo

Manufacturing (-ture)	New Bern	Battle of Moores Creek Bridge	County (-ies)	Kitty Hawk
Mount Mitchell	Charlotte	Bath	James Polk	Tuscarora
Outer Banks	Pamlico Sound		Andrew Johnson	Gold
Tidewater	Battle of Bentonville	Union	Durham	Cherokee
Jefferson Davis	Sir Walter Raleigh	Catawba	River(s)	University of North Carolina

North Carolina Bingo

Sir Walter Raleigh	Border(s)	Raleigh	Cherokee	County (-ies)
Mount Mitchell	Tidewater	Climate	Inner Banks	Battle of Bentonville
Battle of Moores Creek Bridge	University of North Carolina		Motto	Great Dismal Swamp
Andrew Johnson	Kitty Hawk	Plantation	Wilmington	Edward B. Dudley
Edenton Tea Party	Durham	Tuscarora	Manufacturing (-ture)	Outer Banks

North Carolina Bingo

Blackbeard	New Bern	Andrew Jackson	Kitty Hawk	University of North Carolina
Legislative Branch	Raleigh	Edward B. Dudley	Bath	Tuscarora
James Polk	Jefferson Davis		Charlotte	Inner Banks
Durham	Nickname	Wilmington	Catawba	Battle of Moores Creek Bridge
Mountain Region	Cherokee	Plantation	Outer Banks	Executive Branch

North Carolina Bingo: Card No. 6

North Carolina Bingo

Plantation	New Bern	Great Dismal Swamp	Tidewater	Edenton Tea Party
Mountain Region	Kitty Hawk	Great Smoky Mountains	Battle of Bentonville	Mount Mitchell
University of North Carolina	Gold		Inner Banks	Charlotte
Manufacturing (-ture)	Pamlico Sound	Climate	Trail of Tears	Coastal Plain
Durham	County (-ies)	Wilmington	Catawba	Blackbeard

North Carolina Bingo: Card No. 7

North Carolina Bingo

Outer Banks	New Bern	Fort Bragg	Legislative Branch	Charlotte
Mount Mitchell	Battle of Moores Creek Bridge	James Polk	University of North Carolina	Cherokee
Executive Branch	County (-ies)		Kitty Hawk	Border(s)
River(s)	Manufacturing (-ture)	Trail of Tears	Jefferson Davis	Coastal Plain
Union	Durham	Catawba	Raleigh	Mountain Region

North Carolina Bingo: Card No. 8

North Carolina Bingo

Inner Banks	Edenton Tea Party	Great Smoky Mountains	Executive Branch	County (-ies)
Jefferson Davis	Kitty Hawk	Outer Banks	Raleigh	New Bern
Great Seal	Plantation		Battle of Bentonville	Fort Bragg
Edward B. Dudley	Border(s)	Nickname	Motto	Great Dismal Swamp
Pamlico Sound	Wilmington	Climate	Trail of Tears	Andrew Johnson

North Carolina Bingo

Trail of Tears	Legislative Branch	Charlotte	James Polk	Executive Branch
University of North Carolina	Cherokee	Bath	Battle of Bentonville	Kitty Hawk
County (-ies)	New Bern		Gold	Coastal Plain
Nickname	Andrew Johnson	Edward B. Dudley	Wilmington	Great Seal
Climate	Mountain Region	Andrew Jackson	Sir Walter Raleigh	Outer Banks

North Carolina Bingo

Blackbeard	New Bern	Raleigh	Edward B. Dudley	Mountain Region
Fort Bragg	Great Seal	Motto	Inner Banks	Bath
Mount Mitchell	Kitty Hawk		Andrew Jackson	Great Smoky Mountains
Climate	Tuscarora	Wilmington	County (-ies)	Trail of Tears
Jefferson Davis	Durham	Plantation	Catawba	Edenton Tea Party

North Carolina Bingo: Card No. 11

North Carolina Bingo

Edenton Tea Party	Border(s)	Great Seal	Legislative Branch	Inner Banks
Great Smoky Mountains	Mountain Region	Battle of Moores Creek Bridge	Catawba	Battle of Bentonville
Plantation	Great Dismal Swamp		University of North Carolina	James Polk
Durham	Pamlico Sound	Kitty Hawk	Trail of Tears	Mount Mitchell
New Bern	Fort Bragg	County (-ies)	Jefferson Davis	Cherokee

North Carolina Bingo: Card No. 12

North Carolina Bingo

Edward B. Dudley	Border(s)	Blackbeard	Great Seal	University of North Carolina
Battle of Moores Creek Bridge	Fort Bragg	Kitty Hawk	Inner Banks	Coastal Plain
Judicial Branch	Cherokee		Great Smoky Mountains	Great Dismal Swamp
Outer Banks	Wilmington	County (-ies)	Charlotte	Trail of Tears
Durham	Andrew Johnson	Catawba	Plantation	Motto

North Carolina Bingo

Flag	Kitty Hawk	Raleigh	Inner Banks	Jefferson Davis
Cherokee	Plantation	Great Seal	Battle of Bentonville	New Bern
Edward B. Dudley	Gold		Andrew Jackson	Climate
Andrew Johnson	Wilmington	County (-ies)	Charlotte	Blackbeard
Durham	James Polk	Coastal Plain	Mountain Region	Outer Banks

North Carolina Bingo: Card No. 14

North Carolina Bingo

Motto	Inner Banks	Raleigh	Edenton Tea Party	Legislative Branch
Blackbeard	Andrew Jackson	Bath	Battle of Moores Creek Bridge	Jefferson Davis
University of North Carolina	Plantation		Tuscarora	New Bern
Durham	Great Seal	Fort Bragg	Wilmington	Edward B. Dudley
Mountain Region	Pamlico Sound	Catawba	Executive Branch	Great Smoky Mountains

North Carolina Bingo

Charlotte	Great Seal	Fort Bragg	Executive Branch	Piedmont
James Polk	Coastal Plain	Great Dismal Swamp	Mount Mitchell	Gold
Edward B. Dudley	Border(s)		University of North Carolina	Great Smoky Mountains
Manufacturing (-ture)	Cherokee	Durham	Motto	Trail of Tears
Jefferson Davis	Roanoke Island	Catawba	Pamlico Sound	New Bern

North Carolina Bingo

Climate	Research Triangle	Judicial Branch	Great Seal	Flag
Motto	Jefferson Davis	Wilmington	Gold	Great Dismal Swamp
Inner Banks	Outer Banks		Roanoke Island	Fort Bragg
Andrew Johnson	Mountain Region	Trail of Tears	Raleigh	Coastal Plain
Nickname	Edward B. Dudley	Edenton Tea Party	Legislative Branch	Border(s)

North Carolina Bingo

Executive Branch	County (-ies)	Cherokee	Edward B. Dudley	James Polk
New Bern	Climate	Nickname	University of North Carolina	Jefferson Davis
Inner Banks	Coastal Plain		Judicial Branch	Battle of Moores Creek Bridge
Border(s)	Bath	Wilmington	Trail of Tears	Andrew Jackson
Roanoke Island	Great Seal	Raleigh	Research Triangle	Blackbeard

North Carolina Bingo

University of North Carolina	Blackbeard	Great Seal	Fort Bragg	Trail of Tears
Motto	Legislative Branch	New Bern	Edenton Tea Party	Gold
Research Triangle	County (-ies)		Battle of Bentonville	Tuscarora
Andrew Jackson	Roanoke Island	Nickname	Pamlico Sound	Judicial Branch
Battle of Moores Creek Bridge	Piedmont	Mountain Region	Outer Banks	Catawba

North Carolina Bingo

Flag	Research Triangle	Legislative Branch	Great Seal	Catawba
Cherokee	Great Smoky Mountains	Mount Mitchell	Nickname	James Polk
Border(s)	Great Dismal Swamp		Manufacturing (-ture)	Bath
Sir Walter Raleigh	Union	River(s)	Pamlico Sound	Roanoke Island
Tidewater	Outer Banks	Piedmont	Trail of Tears	Judicial Branch

North Carolina Bingo

Motto	Blackbeard	Mount Mitchell	Great Seal	Sir Walter Raleigh
Border(s)	Judicial Branch	Charlotte	Fort Bragg	Plantation
Coastal Plain	Mountain Region		Research Triangle	Raleigh
Nickname	Edenton Tea Party	Roanoke Island	Andrew Johnson	Outer Banks
Manufacturing (-ture)	Piedmont	Catawba	Climate	Pamlico Sound

North Carolina Bingo

Executive Branch	Andrew Jackson	Judicial Branch	Battle of Moores Creek Bridge	Edward B. Dudley
James Polk	Legislative Branch	Tuscarora	Fort Bragg	Battle of Bentonville
Cherokee	Gold		Plantation	Great Dismal Swamp
Roanoke Island	Andrew Johnson	Pamlico Sound	Bath	Mount Mitchell
Piedmont	Climate	Research Triangle	Coastal Plain	Manufacturing (-ture)

North Carolina Bingo: Card No. 22

North Carolina Bingo

Charlotte	Research Triangle	Edenton Tea Party	Battle of Moores Creek Bridge	Catawba
Blackbeard	Flag	Mountain Region	Motto	Bath
Andrew Jackson	Edward B. Dudley		River(s)	Plantation
Coastal Plain	Piedmont	Roanoke Island	Climate	Pamlico Sound
Sir Walter Raleigh	Union	Outer Banks	Nickname	Judicial Branch

North Carolina Bingo: Card No. 23

North Carolina Bingo

Charlotte	Outer Banks	Flag	Research Triangle	Fort Bragg
Judicial Branch	Catawba	Mount Mitchell	James Polk	Plantation
Great Dismal Swamp	Executive Branch		Edward B. Dudley	Coastal Plain
Sir Walter Raleigh	River(s)	Roanoke Island	Climate	Border(s)
Tidewater	Manufacturing (-ture)	Piedmont	Legislative Branch	Union

North Carolina Bingo

Manufacturing (-ture)	Mount Mitchell	Research Triangle	Raleigh	Judicial Branch
Bath	Border(s)	Motto	Charlotte	Battle of Bentonville
Andrew Johnson	Fort Bragg		River(s)	Roanoke Island
Tuscarora	Sir Walter Raleigh	Union	Piedmont	Gold
Catawba	Flag	Cherokee	Jefferson Davis	Tidewater

North Carolina Bingo: Card No. 25

North Carolina Bingo

Judicial Branch	Research Triangle	Andrew Jackson	James Polk	Executive Branch
Nickname	Legislative Branch	Fort Bragg	Flag	Charlotte
Andrew Johnson	River(s)		Gold	Manufacturing (-ture)
Climate	Battle of Moores Creek Bridge	Sir Walter Raleigh	Piedmont	Roanoke Island
Great Dismal Swamp	Jefferson Davis	Raleigh	Union	Tidewater

North Carolina Bingo

Andrew Jackson	Cherokee	Research Triangle	Flag	Great Smoky Mountains
Sir Walter Raleigh	River(s)	Motto	Roanoke Island	Battle of Bentonville
Wilmington	Union		Piedmont	Manufacturing (-ture)
Executive Branch	Blackbeard	Mount Mitchell	Tidewater	Bath
Jefferson Davis	Gold	Judicial Branch	Tuscarora	Great Dismal Swamp

North Carolina Bingo: Card No. 27

North Carolina Bingo

Andrew Jackson	Flag	Tuscarora	Research Triangle	Charlotte
Great Smoky Mountains	Judicial Branch	River(s)	James Polk	Gold
Union	Coastal Plain		Great Dismal Swamp	Nickname
Trail of Tears	Executive Branch	Mountain Region	Piedmont	Roanoke Island
Battle of Moores Creek Bridge	Inner Banks	Jefferson Davis	Tidewater	Sir Walter Raleigh

North Carolina Bingo

Judicial Branch	Flag	Executive Branch	Motto	Inner Banks
Pamlico Sound	Nickname	Mount Mitchell	Great Dismal Swamp	Tuscarora
Andrew Johnson	River(s)		Battle of Bentonville	Research Triangle
Great Smoky Mountains	Sir Walter Raleigh	Kitty Hawk	Piedmont	Roanoke Island
Charlotte	Fort Bragg	Tidewater	Blackbeard	Union

North Carolina Bingo: Card No. 29

North Carolina Bingo

Judicial Branch	Flag	Executive Branch	Motto	Inner Banks
Pamlico Sound	Nickname	Mount Mitchell	Great Dismal Swamp	Tuscarora
Andrew Johnson	River(s)		Battle of Bentonville	Research Triangle
Great Smoky Mountains	Sir Walter Raleigh	Kitty Hawk	Piedmont	Roanoke Island
Charlotte	Fort Bragg	Tidewater	Blackbeard	Union

North Carolina Bingo: Card No. 30